First World War
and Army of Occupation
War Diary
France, Belgium and Germany

74 (YEOMANRY) DIVISION
229 Infantry Brigade,
Brigade Trench Mortar Battery
1 May 1918 - 27 December 1918

WO95/3152/5

The Naval & Military Press Ltd
www.nmarchive.com
Published in association with The National Archives

Published by

The Naval & Military Press Ltd

Unit 10 Ridgewood Industrial Park,
Uckfield, East Sussex,
TN22 5QE England
Tel: +44 (0) 1825 749494

www.naval-military-press.com
www.nmarchive.com

This diary has been reprinted in facsimile from the original. Any imperfections are inevitably reproduced and the quality may fall short of modern type and cartographic standards.

© Crown Copyright
Images reproduced by permission of The National Archives, London, England, 2015.

Contents

Document type	Place/Title	Date From	Date To
Heading	WO95/3152/5 Brigade Trench Mortar Battery		
Heading	74th Division 229th Infy Bde Trench Mortar Battery 1918 May-Dec 1918		
War Diary	A Camp Gabbari Alexandria H.M.T. Ixion	01/05/1918	11/05/1918
War Diary	Marseilles	11/05/1918	13/05/1918
War Diary	Noyelles	15/05/1918	16/05/1918
War Diary	Le Hamelet	16/05/1918	20/05/1918
War Diary	Sq U.8.a. Humbercourt	20/05/1918	21/05/1918
War Diary	Liencourt Sq I.32.d	25/05/1918	26/06/1918
War Diary	Fontes Sq N. 29 C	26/06/1918	10/07/1918
War Diary	Ham-En-Artois Sq. O.27c	11/07/1918	11/07/1918
War Diary	Sq O.34 C	12/07/1918	31/07/1918
War Diary	Ref Map P.27b 1.3	01/08/1918	09/08/1918
War Diary	P7 C 7 8	10/08/1918	16/08/1918
War Diary	Ref. Map 1/40,0000 36a Sq O.34.c	16/08/1918	18/08/1918
War Diary	Ref Map 36A.SE 1/20,000	24/08/1918	24/08/1918
War Diary	Ref. Map 36A 1:40,000	27/08/1918	28/08/1918
War Diary	Ref Map 62d. 1:40,000	28/08/1918	31/08/1918
War Diary	Ref Map 62 C N W 1.20,000 Ed 4b	01/09/1918	04/09/1918
War Diary	Ref Map 62 C N E 1:20000 Ed 5a	06/09/1918	25/09/1918
War Diary	Ref Map 62 D 1:40000 Ed 2a	25/09/1918	28/09/1918
War Diary	Bourec Vic	02/10/1918	04/10/1918
War Diary	Ref Map 36 S W 1:20,000	04/10/1918	16/10/1918
War Diary	Ref Map 36 SE 1:20,000	17/10/1918	19/10/1918
War Diary	Sheet 37 1:20,000	19/10/1918	30/10/1918
War Diary	Camphin Farm M.36.b.2.0	01/11/1918	05/11/1918
War Diary	Lamain N.33 B 8.4	09/11/1918	09/11/1918
War Diary	Beclers Q.14.a.0.5	10/11/1918	10/11/1918
War Diary	Lahamaide B.25.d.3.9	11/11/1918	11/11/1918
War Diary	Wannebecq C 26c 6 8	12/11/1918	12/11/1918
War Diary	Mainvault H.31.b.8.7	17/11/1918	18/11/1918
War Diary	Leuze R 35a5.8	19/11/1918	11/12/1918
War Diary	Lahamaide B.25.d.3.9	15/12/1918	15/12/1918
War Diary	Gremmont V.2.a.5.5	16/12/1918	27/12/1918

WO95/3152/5
Brigade Trench Mortar Battery

74TH DIVISION
229TH INFY BDE

TRENCH MORTAR BATTERY
1918 MAY - DEC 1918

Army Form C. 2118.

WAR DIARY
or
INTELLIGENCE SUMMARY.
(Erase heading not required.)

Instructions regarding War Diaries and Intelligence Summaries are contained in F. S. Regs., Part II. and the Staff Manual respectively. Title pages will be prepared in manuscript.

May 1918

229th We Do. LIGHT TRENCH Mortar Battery

Place	Date	Hour	Summary of Events and Information	Remarks and references to Appendices
	1919		May 1919	
At Sea, Offshore Alexandria	May 1st		Battery embarked on Ship "N". (H.M.T. "IXION") with 230th + 231st L.T.M Batteries	
H.M.T. "IXION"	" 1st	2pm	Capt. P. KENYON SLANEY M.C. being in Command of the 3 Batteries	
	" 3rd		MAJOR GILES OATS. R.G.A (T.F) in command of the troops on board the ship	
			7½ M(?) dum T.M Battery and the 3 L.T.M Batteries grouped for disciplinary	
			purposes whilst on board the ship.	
	" 7th		LIEUT A.H. RENSHAW, 2nd Lt R.L.WHITE and 2nd LT D.A PEEBLES and 4 O.Rs disembark	
			from H.M.T. KAISER-I-HIND Ship G, at MARSEILLES, remainder for the night	
			at No. 8 Rest Camp	
	" 8		LIEUT A.H. RENSHAW 2nd LT R.L WHITE 2nd LT D.A. PEEBLES and 4 ORs entrained	
	" 10-4pm		LIEUT A.H. RENSHAW, 2nd LT R.L WHITE, 2nd LT D.A PEEBLES and 4 O.Rs detrained at	
			NOYELLES, proceeding to the Rest Camp next morning 11th, then	
			proceeding to LE HAMELET	
MARSEILLES	" 11th		1 O.R. admitted to Ship's Hospital	
			Ship arrived at MARSEILLES. Battery disembarked in the afternoon and	
			proceeded to No. 8 Rest Camp.	
	" 13th		Battery entrained proceeding North	
Ref. Map. ABBEVILLE Sheet 1H. Scale 1:100,000				
NOYELLES	" 15th-16th		Battery detrained at NOYELLES, 230th + 231st Batteries entrained to Battery Commanders. Camped to the night at NOYELLES Rest Camp	
LE HAMELET			Battery proceeded from NOYELLES Rest Camp to Billets at LE HAMELET	

Army Form C. 2118.

WAR DIARY
or
INTELLIGENCE SUMMARY.
(Erase heading not required.)

Instructions regarding War Diaries and Intelligence Summaries are contained in F.S. Regs., Part II. and the Staff Manual respectively. Title pages will be prepared in manuscript.

Place	Date	Hour	Summary of Events and Information	Remarks and references to Appendices
Le Hamlet	1918 May 20th		2 O.R.s admitted to Hospital - Sick. Battery entrained at Rue.	W.D.
Ref Map 51c Ordnance Survey April 1917 Edition 2, Scale 1:40000	"			
Sq U.8.a Humbercourt	20-24th		Battery detrained at Ligny St Flochel Sq B.6.a and marched to Billets at Humbercourt, Sq U.8.a.	W.D.
Liencourt Sq I.32.d	25th		Battery marched from Humbercourt Sq U.8.a to Liencourt Sq I.32.d.	W.D.
	27th		Inspection of Battery by General Officer Commanding 74th (Yeo) Division. 2nd Lt D.A. Reeves having completed 18 months Commissioned service was recommended for promotion to Lieutenant.	W.D.
	28th		2nd Lt R.L. White promoted to Lieutenant 5-3-18, see "London Gazette" 9/10/17 Battery Gas N.C.O. proceeded to Agnes Les Duisans for 4 days Gas Course at IV Corps Gas School.	W.D.
	"		1 O.R. taken on Effective Strength to replace 1 O.R. to Hospital.	W.D.
	30th		1 O.R. proceeded to U.K. on one months reengagement leave	W.D.

Bélange Harry
Capt.
O.C. 229th Inf. Bde.
T.M. Battery

WAR DIARY or INTELLIGENCE SUMMARY

229/L.T.M.13/ JUNE 18

Army Form C.2118.

Place	Date	Hour	Summary of Events and Information	Remarks and references to Appendices
REF. MAP. 51c LIENCOURT, Sq 132.d	1918 June 1st		Ordnance Survey April 1917, Edition 2, Scale 1:40000 JUNE 1918 "B" Team earmarked in view of possible move and subsequent operations Battery took part in an Inter-Brigade Tactical Scheme	
	1st		2 O.R's taken on strength to replace casualties	
	"		1 N.C.O. returned from three days Gas course at XVII Corps Gas School	
	2nd		LIEUT. D.A.PEEBLES and 1 N.C.O. commenced course of Instruction in Physical and Bayonet Training at 229th Brigade Headquarters	
	3rd		LIEUTS. A.H.RENSHAW and R.L.WHITE proceeded for a tour in the line with the New Zealand Division	
	4th		CAPT. P. KENYON SLANEY M.C. attended a lecture on co-operation of Tanks and Infantry by G.O.C. 1st Tank Brigade at AVESNES-LE-COMTE 1 O.R. antedate to Establishment appointed for water duty	
	5th		LIEUTS. A.H.RENSHAW and R.L.WHITE proceeded returned from tour in the line	
	6th		1 O.R. proceeded to United Kingdom on one months re-engagement leave	
	"		1 O.R. proceeded to a Brigade Tactical Scheme, the Battery representing the enemy	
	7th		Battery took part in a Brigade Tactical Scheme, the Battery representing the enemy	
	9th		Battery held in readiness to move at six hours notice.	
	12th		1 N.C.O. proceeded to XVIII Corps Gas School for three days course of Instruction	
	13th		1 O.R. proceeded to United Kingdom on 14 days ordinary leave	
	"		Battery held in readiness to move at 18 hours notice	
	"		Field General Court Martial held on 2 O.R's	
	14th		LIEUT. R.L. WHITE proceeded to G.H.Q. Lewis Guns and Light Trench Mortar School Le TOUQUET, for course of Instruction	
	15th		Battery took part in an Inter-Brigade Tactical Scheme	
	16th		2 O.R's admitted to hospital - sick	

Army Form C. 2118.

WAR DIARY
or
INTELLIGENCE SUMMARY.
(Erase heading not required.)

Place	Date	Hour	Summary of Events and Information	Remarks and references to Appendices
Ref Map 57c Ordnance Survey, April 1917, Edition 2, Scale 1:40000			June 1918 (Continued)	
LIGNECOURT A.I.32.d	1918 June 17		1 O.R. admitted to Hospital - sick	J.C.L.
	18th		2 O.Rs. admitted to Hospital - sick	J.C.L.
	"		2 O.Rs. taken on effective strength to replace casualties	J.C.L.
	"		LIEUT D.A. PEEBLES admitted to Hospital - sick	J.C.L.
	"		Battery carried out line firing practice with 3" Stokes ammunition on Sgt O.Y.a. 191 rounds/shell were fired.	J.C.L.
	19th		CAPT H. KENYON SLANEY M.C. proceeded to United Kingdom on 14 days ordinary leave	J.C.L.
	"		LIEUT A.H. RENSHAW assumed command of the Battery	J.C.L.
	20th		2nd LT. J.C. LOUTET, 14th R.H., temporarily attached for duty	J.C.L.
	"		LIEUT A.H. RENSHAW, LANARK YEO and 11 O.Rs. rested to 12th R.S.E.	J.C.L.
	"		2nd LT. J.C. LOUTET assumed command of the Battery	J.C.L.
	21st		2nd LT W.S. HAMBLYN 4th (Res) Som L.I. temporarily attached for duty.	J.C.L.
	"		1 O.R. proceeded to United Kingdom for cadets course for a commission.	J.C.L.
	23rd		17 O.Rs. taken on effective strength to replace casualties and 11 O.Rs. rested to 12th R.S.E.	J.C.L.
	25th		Live firing practice carried out with 3" Stokes ammunition on Sgt O.Y.a.	J.C.L.
	"		42 rounds more fired.	
	26th		1 O.R. proceeded to U.K. for 14 days ordinary leave.	J.C.L.
	"	515 a.m.	Battery moved to new billeting area, entraining at LIGNY ST FLOCHEL	J.C.L.
			Sgt B.L.A.	

WAR DIARY
or
INTELLIGENCE SUMMARY

Army Form C. 2118.

Place	Date	Hour	Summary of Events and Information	Remarks and references to Appendices
REF MAP FRANCE, 36A FONTES Sq. N.29 c			JUNE 1918 (Continued) EDITION 6. Scale 1:40000	
	June 26		Battery detrained at AIRE Sq. H.29.b. and marched to billets at FONTES, N.29.c. Battery held in readiness to move to reinforce the line at the following notice:— Donkey between 5.30 a.m. and 7.30 a.m. at 1½ hours notice, otherwise at 3 hours notice.	JCL
	27th		Orders received that on the command to move, the Battery to proceed to Sq. O. 36. a. 8.8.	JCL
	"		Reconnaissance of the emergency switch line carried out. Gun positions selected — 4 guns covering drawbridge in P.20 Central; 4 guns in P.8.a. + b.	JCL
	28th		Orders received that on the command "Man Battle Positions", the Battery to move to vicinity of LA PIERRIERE (P.19.a) and remain there in reserve.	JCL

J. Lauter Capt.
O.C. 229th Inf. Bde.
T.M. Battery

WAR DIARY or INTELLIGENCE SUMMARY

Army Form C. 2118.

July 1918

229th T.M. Battery

Place	Date	Hour	Summary of Events and Information	Remarks and references to Appendices
Ref Map. FRANCE, 36A Edition 6, 1:40000			JULY 1918	
Fouquières sq M.12	July 1/2		Reconnaissance of the BUSNES – STEENBECQUE – AMUSOIRES – HAVERSQUERQUE and LILLERS – STEENBECQUE lines carried out.	M.
	6		"C" 01% forwarded to St Pols School for L.T.M. course	M.
	10		"B" Section proceeded to 57th Division Reception Camp WITTERNESSE	M.
Plumer Park sq O.21.c	11		229th Bde Rolief 130th Bde in Drummond Camp. The battery relieving	M.
			130th Battery at HAM-EN-ARTOIS Sq O.21.c	
Sq O.21.c	12		Daylight recce of front Source O.21.c Sq O.21.c	M.
	13		Recce of L.B.M. Emplacements in the trenches on the Sherpenberg	M.
	19		Bombing barrage by O.I.B. reorganised	
Plumer Park sq O.21.c			"B" Section returned from 57th Division Reception Camp WITTERNESSE	
	20		Gas Strafe on Mont Noire Battle Position carried out	
			36th S.F. Edition 8A 1:20,000	M.
	25		"B" Section proceeded to 74th Division Reception Camp WITTERNESSE	M.
			Battery relieved 230 LTM Battery in the Line Right completed at	M.
			7.45 p.m. Battery headquarters at P.24.c.1.3. Forward Headquarters	M.
			at P.24.c. 82.97. Gun Positions Q.13.d.99.13, Q.13.d.98.20, Q.19.a.85.25	
			and Q.19.a.85.30. Alternative Emplacements Q.19.a.40.80 and Q.19.a.45.75	
			Reserve Emplacements P.24.c.90.09, P.24.c.61.20, P.30.a.59.84, P.30.a.57.85	
			Plumer – Remy	

WAR DIARY
or
INTELLIGENCE SUMMARY.
(Erase heading not required.)

Army Form C. 2118.

Place	Date	Hour	Summary of Events and Information	Remarks and references to Appendices
	July 28–31st		Working parties daily to and from digging pits and improving gun positions	
	29		Guns again silenced	
	31		Gun teams relieved	

Henry Slaney Capt.
O.C. 229th H⁺ Bde.
T.M. Battery

Army Form C. 2118.

229th T.M. Battery

WAR DIARY
or
INTELLIGENCE SUMMARY.
(Erase heading not required.)

Instructions regarding War Diaries and Intelligence Summaries are contained in F. S. Regs., Part II. and the Staff Manual respectively. Title pages will be prepared in manuscript.

Place	Date	Hour	Summary of Events and Information	Remarks and references to Appendices
Ref Map. 36 A SE 1/20,000 Edition 8A	August 1915			
P24b.13	Aug 1st		Battery Headquarters at LABIETTE FARM Sq P.24.b.13	
	"	1-3rd	Working parties daily improving gun positions and digging pits.	
	"	5	1 OR admitted to Hospital - Sick	
	"	8	" " " " " "	
	"	8	Owing to enemy withdrawal Battery H.Q. moved forward to Advanced Bde H.Q. P.24.c.82.94	
	"		Right Section (2 guns) moved forward from B.94. a.25.30 to Q.10.d.4.7 Left Section (2 guns)	
	"		moved from Sq Q.13.d.99.13 and Q.13.d.98.20 to Q.10.a.6.7	
	"		Carrying parties of 50 ORs attached from 16th Devon Regt while Battery in the line	
	"	9	2 OR killed and 3 OR wounded by shell fire.	
	"	9	Right Section (2 guns) moved from Q.10.d.4.7 to Q.10.c.9.4	
P7 c y 8.	" 10		Battery relieved, 2 guns remaining in the line attached 230th T.M. Battery	
	"		Battery moved to neighbourhood of LABIETTE FARM P.24.c.y.8	
	"		attached 230th T.M./B.4	
	" 16		2 remaining guns in the line relieved, Brigade came into Divisional Reserve	
Ref Map. Ha0000 36 A Sq Q.34.c	"		and Battery proceeded to HAM-EN-ARTOIS Sq Q.34.c	
	"		"B" Echelon rejoined Battery	
	18		Battery attended Brigade Service Parade and Inspection by Army Commander	

WAR DIARY
or
INTELLIGENCE SUMMARY.

Army Form C. 2118.

Place	Date	Hour	Summary of Events and Information	Remarks and references to Appendices
Ref Map 1/40000 361			2	
Sq. Q.31.c Aug 18			4 OR's taken on effective strength to replace casualties	
Ref Map 1/40000 Sh.57c ASE	Aug 24		231st T.M. Battery relieved 22 Battery on the Line. Battery H.Q. at CAVIN FARM Sq. R.24.d.45.45. Gun Positions — Right Section Q.10.c. 40.40. Left Section (2 guns) K.35.d.9.6.	M
Ref Map 36A 1/40000	Aug 27		Battery relieved in the Line by 174th T.M. Battery. Battery proceeded to HAMMEN-ARTAIS. Sq. O.27.c.	M
	" 28		Battery entrained at BERGUETTE.	M
Ref Map 62D 1/40000	29		" detrained at CORBIE Sq. O.5.a. and proceeded to BÉHENCOURT Sq. B.18.d.	M
	" 28		1 OR proceeded to U.K. for London Course of Instruction.	M
	" 30		2nd Lt. R.L. WHITE, K.O. Norfolk Yeo, granted extension of leave as U.K. restored of strength (Auth.) M.B. 138-18. Unfit A Person B. 2 mos Per C.Y.	M
	" 31		74th Division proceeded to relieve 58th Division. Battery embussed at FRANVILLERS, debussing near MARICOURT.	M

A.6945 Wt. W11422/M1160 350,000 12/16 D.D. & L. Forms/C/2118/14.

WAR DIARY or INTELLIGENCE SUMMARY

(Erase heading not required.)

Army Form C. 2118.

Place	Date	Hour	Summary of Events and Information	Remarks and references to Appendices
			SEPTEMBER, 1918	
REF MAP 62 c. N.W.1. 20000 Ed 4B	Aug 31		Battery marched from debussing point near MARICOURT and bivouaced in trench on B.25.b.	MP
	Sept 1	Morning	Moved to Etu at B.22.a. Moved forward at 2.30 pm to g C.20.a near BUCHAVESNES	MP
	2	Afternoon	Sections moved forward and guns mounted – Right Section (2 guns) in C.24.d.9.9 and Left Section (2 guns) in C.16.c.	MP
	2		1 OR wounded	VM
	3-4		Left Section moved into position at C.23.b. 3.4. Right Section moved to C.21.c.8.6	PP
	4		1 N.C.O. for details leave for Commission to UK	MP
	5	Evening	Battery withdrawn from the line and moved to H.5.b.9.0.	MP
REF MAP 62 c NE 1. 1.20.000 Ed 5A	6	Evening	Battery moved to AIZECOURT J.1.d.3.0	MP
	7	Afternoon	Battery moved to trench in neighbourhood of LONGAVESNES K.1.a.1.2	PP
	8-9		Moved to VILLERS FAUCON. E.29.b.	PP
	10-11		Moved to trench K.1.a.1.2	SP
	11		1 NCO proceeded to UK for details leave for Commission	SP
	12	Evening	Battery moved to FAUSTIN QUARRY K.5.d./3	DP
	20-21		Guns in position in support – Right Section at CONNOR POST F.18.d.3.4. Left Section at ORCHARD POST F.22.c./3	ML

Army Form C. 2118.

WAR DIARY
or
INTELLIGENCE SUMMARY.
(Erase heading not required.)

Place	Date	Hour	Summary of Events and Information	Remarks and references to Appendices
REF MAP 62.c.N.E. 1/20000 Ed. 5A	Sept.			
	21-22		Battery moved to TEMPLEUX LE GERARD A.13.b.1.8. QUARRIES	
	22		3 O.R's wounded. 1 OR gassed.	
	22-23		Battery relieved 230th & 231st Batteries on the Line, Right Section relieving 230th TMB at RIFLEMAN POST F.29.b.6.3 and Left Section relieving 231st TMB at BENJAMIN POST F.29.b.4.4.	
	23-24		1 Gun - Right Section - moved to ZOGCA TRENCH F.30.a.8.4.	
	24-25		Battery withdrawn from the line and proceeded to FAUSTIN QUARRY K.5.d.1.3	
	25 Morning		" entrained at TINCOURT Sq. J.24.	
REF. MAP 62.d. 1/40000 Ed. 2				
	25		Detrained at VILLERS BRETONNEUX O.36 and marched to CORBIE Sq. A.5	
	26		"B" team rejoined Battery	
	27		Entrained at MERICOURT L'ABBÉ Sq. J.9	
	28		Detrained at BERGUETTE O.15.d. and marched to BOURECQ U.1.c.	

Akuya Gary Capt.
O.C. 230th Inf. Bde.
T.M. Battery

Army Form C. 2118.

WAR DIARY
or
INTELLIGENCE SUMMARY.
(Erase heading not required.)

Place	Date	Hour	Summary of Events and Information	Remarks and references to Appendices
			OCTOBER 1918	
REF MAP 36a	Oct 2	14000 Edr	Battery moved from BOUREC - Battery to BURBURE N23a & 9 proceeding from the to LONG CORNET N23a 98 by light Railway	
BOUREC VIC				
REF MAP 36SW	" 4	H 1700 N24 c 00	Special from LONG CORNET to N9 43 5	
			1 OR returned from General Leave to United Kingdom	
	" 5		1 Offr 1 OR proceeded on 14 days General Leave to United Kingdom	
	" 6		1 NCO proceeded to XI Corps Gas School for Course	
	" 7		1 OR admitted to Field Ambulance & 1 OR returned from hospital	
	" 8		Lt E. LUND YATES, 2nd Bn Hamps Regt attd 16th Devon Regt attd to this Battery for instruction	
			1 OR admitted to Field Ambulance	
	" 9		2 ORs returned from 14 days General Leave to United Kingdom	
	" 10	1400	Battery moved to N24c25	
	" 11	0800	" N23a20 Gresson's place been destroyed by Shell fire	
			" LINEY WOOD N28a 72 (2 Guns) & N28a 41 (2 Guns)	
			4 Guns presented in LINEY WOOD N28a 72 (2 Guns) & N28a 41 (2 Guns)	
			Lt E. LUND YATES admitted to Hospital	
			1 Offr 1 OR returned from XI Corps Gas School from Course	
			1 OR proceeded to XI Corps School for French duties Course	
	" 14		2 Offrs 8 & 20 ORs attached as carrying party from 16th Devon Regt	

WAR DIARY
or
INTELLIGENCE SUMMARY.
(Erase heading not required.)

Army Form C. 2118.

Place	Date	Hour	Summary of Events and Information	Remarks and references to Appendices
			OCTOBER (cont) Sheet 2.	
	Oct 16		Guns moved forward from LINGY WOOD to Railway Embankment on 29gd near road crossing	
			Head Quarters moved to O.8.d.2.2.	M2
	"16		Guns moved up right flanking being billed at FORT HABOURDIN Pya & MASURE Ftn P.25 & 27	M2
		0400	Head Quarters to Rubeley Entrenchment at O.29.b.1.09.	M2
REF MAP 36 SE	"17	0300	moved to O.30.c.1.4. Carrying Party from 16th Devon Regt. returned to Unit.	M2
1/20,000	"18	1016.	Guns & Head Quarters moved to Chateau Q.26.b.3.2.	M2
			1 Off. 22 ORs ran as carrying Party from 19th Somerset Light Infantry	
			2 Gns proceeded on 14 days General Leave to United Kingdom	
			2 GR. returned from 14 days General leave to United Kingdom	M2
	"19		Carrying Party from 19th Somerset L.I. returned to Unit	
SHEET 44		1100	moved to Kennoyes P.15.c.50.35	M2
1/20,000	"20	1600	" " PONT A TRESSIN M.20.d.55	
	"21	1715	" " ENPINE N.2.d.35 (Belgium Frontier)	M2
	"22	1800	2 Guns moved into line at O.26.6.5.4.	M2
23/24			2 Guns in action on targets about FAUBOURG DE LILLE 120 Rounds expected	M2
			Ammunition supply from D.A.F. difficult.	

A0045 Wt. W11942/A1166 350,000 12/16 D. D. & L. Forms/C,/F18/14.

WAR DIARY or INTELLIGENCE SUMMARY

Army Form C. 2118.

Place	Date	Hour	Summary of Events and Information	Remarks and references to Appendices
			OCTOBER 1918 (cont) Sheet 3	
	Oct 24		1 Off. returned from 14 days General Leave to United Kingdom	AF
			1 OR proceeded on 14 days General Leave to United Kingdom	
			Battery relieved by 230 Lt. of S.Battery & proceeded to CAMPHIN AREA M.36.b.2. CALONNE FARM	AF
	28		2 ORs returned from 14 days General Leave to United Kingdom	AF
	29		3 ORs taken on effective strength & 1 OR returned from B.TEAM	PKS
			1 Off & 1 OR attached	
			2 ORs proceeded on 14 days General Leave to United Kingdom	AF
	30		1 OR returned from 14 days General Leave to United Kingdom	
			1 OR returned from hospital	
			1 OR brought under Escort from London area - Absente without Leave.	

1-11-18.

P.Kenyon. Kenyon Capt
O.C. 229th Inf. Bde
T.M. Batty

Army Form C. 2118.

WAR DIARY
or
INTELLIGENCE SUMMARY.

(Erase heading not required.)

229th T.M Battery

Summary of Events and Information

November 1918

Place	Date	Hour	Summary of Events and Information	Remarks and references to Appendices
REF MAP FRANCE SHEET 37 Ed 3 1:40,000				
CAMPHIN FARM M 26.C.2.0	1st - 3rd		Training	
"	4th		Lt R.W. DICKSON 10th attd 14th R.H. permanently attached and taken on effective strength	M3
"	5th		12 ORs attached	A5
LAMAIN N.33.C.84	9th	1000	Battery moved to LAMAIN (Belgium) N 33 C.8.4.	A3
BECLERS Q.14.a.0.5	10th	0800	" Eastward marching through TOURNAI and billeted for the night at BECLERS Q 14.a.0.5	A4
REF MAP FRANCE SHEET 38. ATH. 1:40,000				
LAMAMAIDE B.25.d.3.9.	11th	0900	Battery marched to LAMAMAIDE B 25 d 39	A3
WANNEBECQ C.26.c.6.8.	12th	1100	" moved to WANNEBECQ C 26.c.68	A5
MAINVAULT H.31.A.8.4	14th	0900	" MAINVAULT H 31.A.8.4	A2
"	18th		Capt. P. KENYON-SLANEY MC. appointed Sports Representative to 229th Inf Brigade	A2
REF MAP FRANCE SHEET 37 Ed 3 1:40,000				
LEUZE R.35.a.5.8.	19th	1000	Battery moved to LEUZE R 35 a.5.8	
	19th-30th		Training and working parties	

O Kenyon-Slaney Capt.
O.C. 229th. Inf. Bde.
T.M. Battery

229th T.M Battery

WAR DIARY
or
INTELLIGENCE SUMMARY
(Erase heading not required.)

December 1918

Place	Date	Hour	Summary of Events and Information	Remarks and references to Appendices
Ref. Map Belgium Sheet 34 Ed 3 1:40,000				
Leuze R.35 a.5.8	Dec 1	-		
	4		Educational classes commenced	
	7		H.M. The King passed through Leuze	
	11		4 O.Rs. proceeded to U.K. for Demobilization as coalminers	
Ref Map Belgium Sheet 38 Ath 1:40,000				
Lahamaide B.25 d.3.9	15	0830	Battery commenced march to Grammont, and billeted at Lahamaide B.25 d.3.9	
Ref Map Belgium Sheet 36 Ed 2 1:40,000	15		March continued	
Grammont V.2.a.5.5	16	0900	Battery reaching Grammont V.2 a.5.5 at 1430	
	27	0830	3 O.Rs. proceeded to U.K. for Demobilization as coalminers	
	29		Capt F Kenyon-Slaney M.C. relinquished command of the Battery on being attached to Headquarters 229th Inf. Brigade	
	29		Lieut R.W. Dickson assumed command of the Battery	
	29		2nd Lieut J.C. Loutet proceeded on 14 days leave to U.K.	

O.C. 229th Inf. Bde.
T.M. Battery

www.ingramcontent.com/pod-product-compliance
Lightning Source LLC
Chambersburg PA
CBHW081509160426
43193CB00014B/2636